Copyright © 2023 Sam Johnson

First published in Great Britain in 2023 by SBMoore Publishing.

The right of Sam Johnson to be identified as the Author of the Work has been asserted by him in accordance with the Copyright, Designs and Patents Act 1988.

All rights reserved. No part of this publication may be reproduced, stored in a retrieval system or transmitted in any means, electronic, photocopying, recording or otherwise, without the permission of the publisher.

This book is sold subject to the condition that it shall not, by way of trade or otherwise, be lent, re-sold, hired out or circulated without the publisher's prior consent in any form of binding or cover other than that in which it is published and without similar condition being imposed on the subsequent purchaser.

No responsibility for loss occasioned to any person acting or refraining from action as a result of any material in this publication can be accepted by the author or publisher.

For more information on about discounts for bulk purchases, please contact: sbmoorepublishing@gmail.com

Designed by Sam Johnson

BREAKUP SURVIVAL GUIDE

The survival guide to help you through modern heartbreaks

Dedication

This book is dedicated to anyone going through a breakup or trying to heal from a heartbreak.

Prologue

Everyone experiences heartbreak and break-ups in different ways. This book has been written to help give you some ways to work through the heartbreak you may be currently feeling, whether you were the person that broke off the relationship or you were the person who was broken up with. Now before you start asking about whether there is scientific evidence behind these different activities or tasks, the answer is **NO**. If you are looking for a book that has scientific evidence or goes into the psychological reasoning as to why you feel the way you do, as well as giving you the best way to combat these feelings, then I suggest you stop reading here and give this book to a friend or a charity shop as it will not help you answer those questions.

If you aren't here for any of those things then I hope the activities that I have come up with help you deal with what you are going through. Now you are probably wondering what my credentials are to be writing a book on a matter that everyone goes through, and why you should take any notice of what I have to say. To put it lightly, I wouldn't say I am qualified on the matter of heartbreak nor do I think anyone is. We all experience different things in our relationships, and have relationships for differing durations of time, meaning we are all going to experience different feelings and emotions during any break-ups that we have. The one thing that we all have in common is that we will all need to pick ourselves up after a break-up and try to get on with our lives.

As someone who has gone through a long, drawn out break-up and understands how it feels to be heartbroken, I have written this book as a guide based on what I have experienced in trying to get used to being single again and recover from the heartbreak. You may find some of these activities/tasks might not work for you, but I hope that they help guide you to solutions that do help. I am also a man of very few words so you can guarantee I'm not going to waffle on about nonsense.

So without any more delay, here is my very small survival guide to a break-up *(matches not included)*...

40 things to do when you are heartbroken

Here are 40 things to do when you are heartbroken. These activities range from tasks to help you start moving on from your ex, to helping you get back out there and enjoying single life. As mentioned, I'm not expecting you to go and to do everything in this book (if you do then well done, you are definitely on the way to healing yourself), but just give some of them a go and see if they help you deal with how you are feeling. This list is in no particular order so feel free to skip through and pick-out the ones you feel are relevant to you and that you want to focus on.

Before we start, please remember that no one is expecting you to heal straight away. Everyone heals at their own pace so take your time. This isn't a race against you and your ex, about who can get back into the dating scene and 'live their best life'. It's a chance for you to develop yourself and get to know yourself again, while you go and enjoy your life.

1. Watch some movies

This is probably not what you expected to be at the start of this list, and it may seem like a standard practice to lie in front of the TV binge watching films when you're feeling heartbroken. When I say watch some movies, I mean in the first month or so stay away from every romantic or romcom film, and just focus on the other genres. I personally highly recommend watching a lot of comedies as for the duration of the film you can immerse yourself in something funny and try to feel a bit more 'normal'.

The reason why you should be staying away from romantic films and romcoms in this initial period of grief/heartbreak after the relationship has ended is that you are trying to stop your brain from romanticising the situation that you are in, by thinking that your ex will come back to you like in the movies. Unfortunately this just doesn't happen in real life. There is a reason why your relationship has ended and the healthiest thing for you to do is to move on and try to make the most of your life.

2. Unfollow your ex on all social media

This may be self explanatory, but it will help your mental health and help you move on from this heartbreak a lot quicker if you unfollow them on all forms on social media. Now you may have hoped that you can stay friends and there is nothing stopping you adding them back later on if that is what you want. At the moment though you don't need to be reminded daily of 'all the fun' they are having now they are single. People only post the fun they are having and you aren't going to see them heartbroken.

As hard as it is to read this I don't want to get your hopes up that your ex is heartbroken and is regretting breaking up with you, as it is highly likely they aren't. If your ex was the one to break-up with you then they probably had quite a bit of time to come to terms with the break-up before it even happened, and so they won't be feeling any regret or heartbreak when it finally happens. It is also important to keep in mind that you are only going to hurt yourself further by seeing them out with someone new, so think of yourself and just click that unfollow button.

3. Spend some time and work out who you are

I'm afraid that I am going to be a bit 'deep and real' with this one so please bear with me. During a relationship you may find that you changed who you were in order to fulfil the needs of your partner and to try to be so 'perfect' that they won't leave you. That means that now you are probably feeling a bit lost and not know where you fit in the world or who you are as a person.

This can be extremely daunting and you may feel like you are the only one who feels this way but trust me you're not. What you now need to do is to take some time to work out what you enjoy doing and the values that you want to live by.

I'm not going to sugar coat this one for you and this may take weeks, months or even years to work out. But by going through the process of understanding who you are, you will find that there is a person within who fits with how you want to live your life. Though this isn't going to magically fix how you are feeling about the break-up, it will give you the foundations that you need to grow going forward.

4. Limit your social media use

This is probably blasphemy in this day and age where everyone is online 24/7, but stay with me. You need time to comprehend how you are feeling and time to allow those feelings to fade, and getting a quick dopamine hit from looking at your socials is not going to help. If anything you are just going to get more addicted to your phone as you try and suppress the feelings you are having. So limit yourself when looking at social media and start engaging with the world a bit more; you are more likely to find peace watching a sunset than you are scrolling to see if your friends are out partying without you.

The urge to get onto Instagram or Tiktok can sometimes be overwhelming, especially if you are bored and want to kill 30 minutes before going to bed. In these instances I highly recommend picking up a book or a magazine. Not only will this help you stifle the boredom, but it will also allow you to get absorbed into something that won't damage your eyesight and you won't get that unhealthy dopamine hit.

2.5 hrs
Till you can open Instagram

5. Go for a daily walk

I hope you are reading this in the spring to autumn time when the weather is nice and going for a walk isn't cold and wet. You might be thinking that going for a walk is going to be a bit too much for you at the moment, but to that I say get yourself out of bed and put on some shoes. Not only will the fresh air help you feel a bit more human and alive, it will also make you feel as though you have accomplished something for the day. You don't need to go for a long walk for the benefits; a twenty minute loop around the neighbourhood will help clear your head and make you feel as though you have accomplished something. As well as helping with your mental health, walking is a good way to fit in physical activity should you have a busy life, as you don't need to spend any time getting equipment ready or changing into specific clothing.

6. Buy some new clothes and get a new haircut

Now I can't believe that I'm recommending this one as I'm not one for shopping. However, going out and buying a set of new clothes can help realign yourself with who you are as you would be dressing for yourself and not how someone else wants you to dress. This in turn will help boost your self-confidence and allow you to start becoming this new improved version of yourself. Buying some new clothes is also a good excuse to get yourself out of the house and to meet up with some of your friends so that you are able to show off your latest purchases.

Once you have the new clothes, it's time to get that new haircut you have been thinking about for a while now. You have a chance to re-define who you are, so why not experiment with a new look. I'm not one for complicated haircuts and have gotten a buzz cut for a while now, but I understand the boost in confidence that you can get when you have a fresh trim; as with getting new clothes it can make you feel like a new person. The whole point of getting a new haircut is not to create a false identity, but rather help to solidify who you are as a person. Getting out of a relationship, especially long term ones, can leave you feeling like you've lost your identity. So taking these steps to help define who you are as a person will help you to start to heal from the heartbreak that you are feeling.

7. Meet-up with your friends

You are probably thinking the only thing that will get you through these hard times is a pot of ice-cream and binge watching TV. Doing these things may help you in the short term, however they aren't a good long term solution. The best long-term solution is to meet up with your friends, to go out on the town, or go away on trips.

Getting yourself out around people who enjoy being with you will allow you to start living your life again and having fun. It is important to remind yourself that even though you have lost someone through the break-up process, there are people (outside of your family) who are in your corner. Now this isn't an excuse six months down the line to still be complaining to them about the break-up. It is a chance to talk things through with them in the initial stages so that you can get a better perspective on what your relationship really was like, and help you develop yourself for your future relationships.

8. Plan a holiday

Plan a holiday for yourself! There is no better opportunity than the present to go and catch some sun! This can be either a domestic holiday or an international holiday, but make sure that it is somewhere that you have never been before. The trip you plan can be either a solo trip or with friends/family, but travelling will allow you experience new things and start showing you how much there is out there for you to explore and take advantage of now you are single. It will also allow you to have something to look forward to should you ever feel lonely or down.

Taking yourself on holiday will also show you that just because you aren't in a relationship with anyone anymore it doesn't mean that you need to put your life on hold. You may never know, by taking this holiday you may bump into your next partner or just make new friends to create new adventures with.

9. Join some new groups

I know that the idea of meeting new people can be extremely daunting. I hate the idea of meeting new people, and I am extremely socially awkward in those kinds of situations. However, by pushing yourself to do it you will learn that doing things that scare you can result in making friends you thought you'd never have.

These groups can be doing anything you want, including hobbies you currently do or new hobbies that you wish to try out and had never got around to doing. Getting out and doing these new activities whilst meeting new people will not only help build your confidence in the long run, but you might even find a passion for something that you never thought you had. One of the first things I did in the weeks after my last relationship ended was to go and find a local running group, which meant I knew once a week I could go out and meet new people who were interested in running. It also meant that I had a set time set aside where I could focus on a sport I really enjoy, whilst also starting to fill in this extra free time that had appeared within my schedule.

10. Pull silly faces at yourself in the mirror

This is one of my favourite things to do because it brings out your inner child and seems to work **100% of the time** when I do it. You spend your whole life trying to be 'grown-up' and 'acting your age', but by embracing the silly things in life it can help make everyday boring tasks fun (I kindly ask all psychologists not to look too deeply into this, as it is just a bit of fun).

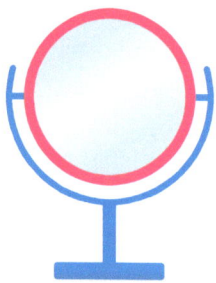

The best way to do this is for maybe 2 seconds when you're washing your hands, or brushing your teeth, or just looking at the outfit you are wearing in the mirror, to pull a funny face at yourself. The first couple of times you do this you will feel stupid and wonder what you are doing, but as you do it more and more you will start to see the funny side of it. Doing this will also allow you to engage with your inner child, and that taking some time just to be yourself can turn any day around, no matter how bad you're feeling.

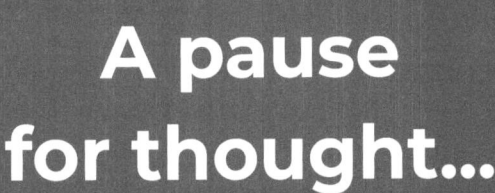

A pause for thought...

This is important and definitely should be one of the things you take away from reading this book. Please stop comparing yourself to where your friends and family members are in life and with their relationships. Everyone has a different path to take through life which means you are all going to achieve different goals at different points. By comparing yourself to friends (especially those who are in relationships) you are only going to make yourself feel bad for a so-called 'step back' in life. However, you haven't taken a step back at all, rather you have gained experience and knowledge of what you want for your next relationship and what you want to do in this next phase of your life. I was placed in this exact spot when I came out of my last relationship. I'd gone from living with someone to having to move back in with my parents at 25 years of age whilst my friends were either moving in with their partners, or were further along with where they wanted to be in life.

Instead of comparing where I was, I took this tiny step back as an opportunity to evaluate where I wanted to be and the type of life I wanted to live. From there I started the long process of building the life that I wanted for myself. I know this is easier said than done, but the only way you can be truly happy is if you stop comparing yourself to others and focus on the path that is in front of you.

11. Join a dating app (18+)

No better way to get over someone and to get your confidence back than joining a dating app and going on some dates. This might seem a bit daunting at first as you will probably have to relearn how to flirt and handle the small talk that comes with dating. However, by starting to date again you will realise that there is someone else out there for you and you never know how much fun you can end up having on these dates.

When starting out please remember not to take rejection or ghosting too personally. Use these rejections as an opportunity to learn what works and what doesn't work. That way you can improve each interaction you have, and get yourself ready for when you are fully ready to jump back into dating someone new.

The one thing I would say to keep in mind before and during the early stages of dating again is that you need to make sure you don't jump in looking for something serious. Use this opportunity to test the water with potential partners and have some fun.

You should make sure you have healed a bit before you get into something serious again, so that you can reduce the likelihood of undoing any of the progress you have made during your healing journey so far. Don't feel like you should be dating straight away after a break-up; everyone heals in different ways and would be ready to jump back into the swing of things at different times. Therefore leaving a long period of time isn't a bad thing and you shouldn't be pressured by people to 'jump back onto the bandwagon'.

12. Learn mindfulness

I know there is a bit of a scepticism around mindfulness and to be honest I wasn't one to think that it would be helpful at all, especially when I was introduced to it in 6th Form (aged 17 for those living outside of the UK). Mindfulness won't stop you from thinking about your ex, or stop you reminiscing about the relationship that you had, but it will help you control those thoughts and feelings, allowing you to deal with them in a healthy way.

Something to keep in mind when practising mindfulness is, as with anything, it needs practice. You aren't going to see results on the first day or weeks of doing it. By keeping with it and developing the skills further, you will see better results in your mental resilience and hopefully develop the skills necessary to manage the thoughts that keep swirling around in your mind.

13. Read some books

We all have a pile or list of books that we 'really should start reading' but have been putting off for a couple of years because we have other things to do (or let's be honest, would much rather scroll through social media). Well now is your chance to get through that list! This doesn't mean you need to be reading all day. Just spending thirty minutes a day can help you relax and immerse yourself in another world.

If you really want to improve yourself after the break-up, use the opportunity to read non-fiction books on a subject that interests you. Not only will this increase your knowledge, but will help serve you while you change into a higher valued version of yourself. If you are someone who really doesn't enjoy reading, then I highly recommend listening to audio books. That way you can listen to something whilst doing other things.

14. Go out for a meal by yourself

This will seem extremely daunting at first but stay with me. There is nothing wrong with going out for a meal by yourself. You can't guarantee that your friends are always going to be free to go out with you and you shouldn't limit yourself to trying new things based on the availability of other people. You will find that if you go out for breakfast, lunch or dinner your confidence in yourself will increase. Now if you're wondering 'what am I supposed to do when I go out by myself?', there is quite a bit you can do including;

- Taking that book that you recently started reading;
- Watch television or a film on your phone;
- People watch!

You shouldn't stop treating yourself to nice meals out just because you are single. Once you get used to eating out alone you will find that you are suddenly able to go to all those restaurants that you wanted to try but that no one else wanted to go to.

15. Have a clear-out

Probably one of the most boring activities to do (unless you enjoy cleaning up, in which case this is just up your alley). Having a clear out of all that junk that has been lying around where you live will allow you to create a more relaxing environment to live in. A big thing that you are going to need to get used to is suddenly having a lot more time on your hands. Try to be productive instead of wasting it on activities that don't fulfil you.

The process of having to sort through things will allow your mind to have time to focus on something else apart from what has just happened to you. You never know, you might end up finding an old piece of junk which could be worth quite a bit of money when sold online.

16. Allow time to embrace your feelings

I promise you this is not some hippie rubbish, so please stay with me. In order to heal from what you have gone through and to grow as a person you need to embrace the fact that you are hurting at the moment. It's completely normal to feel heartbroken for months after a break-up. If however you suppress all these feelings so that you can just 'get back to normal', you will find that you will end up experiencing a lot more pain further down the line when you find you cannot hold them in any longer.

This doesn't mean that you should lie in bed for two months re-watching the same television shows or movies. Rather, acknowledge the fact that you don't feel great today because you're missing your ex (or more importantly missing having someone in your life) and then try to organise something that will make you feel good. I personally really enjoy exercising and I try to make sure that I put a run or a workout at the end of each day so that if I've been feeling down then at least I know I have something enjoyable to look forward to. At the end of the day, you have to remember that you are trying to heal yourself emotionally so that when you get to your next relationship you won't have any baggage with you.

Finally, I think the most important thing that you can do for yourself in the early stages of the break up is to allow yourself time to cry. This is especially important for the men reading this book. There is no shame in crying, and if anyone makes you feel bad for doing so it's best not to hang out with them anymore. I'm not talking about crying all the time, but just to find yourself a safe space and allow five minutes to let all the emotions out. You will find that by doing so you will feel slightly better and be able to think more clearly. Remember, embracing these emotions will help you heal a lot faster than just suppressing your feelings.

17. See a therapist about how you're feeling

As you are experiencing this emotional pain, you will be looking for the best way to deal and overcome it; a therapist will be able to help with that. They will be able to teach you techniques to deal with the emotions you are feeling, as well as helping you explore how to become an independent person again. This approach will not be for everyone and should only be looked at if you feel ready and able to engage with the process.

Counselling is more readily available than it was (and available free via the NHS for UK readers). If you are ill you would go and see a doctor; if you pulled a muscle exercising you would see a physiotherapist. So why not go see a therapist who is trained to help with the mind and emotions? There is no shame in seeking professional help, and you may find that they can give you skills which you can pass on to friends and loved ones when they go through a similar experience.

18. Set yourself a goal

This is a very vague activity because it is up to you to decide what your goal is going to be. The aim isn't to set something that you have no inclination of completing. The whole idea of setting yourself a goal is to firstly have some fun, but also to have something that you can be proud of completing. This will hopefully allow you to focus more on the future rather than continuing to think of what's happened in the past.

Setting a goal will also allow you to become a better version of yourself, because once that goal has been completed you will want to set more goals in order to get the same feeling of accomplishment. This in turn will improve your sense of self worth and will hopefully give you the confidence boost you need to go out and get what you want in life.

Goals to set yourself can include:

- Career related objectives;
- Start a new hobby that has always interested you;
- If you're into sports, completing a race or participating in a match;
- **Or** if you are still feeling a bit overwhelmed, then set a goal to get yourself out of the house once a day to get some fresh air.

19. Start a side-business
(this is not financial advice!)

This is for the people who don't mind increasing their weekly workload and spending a little less time in the club. Starting a side-business is going to be a lot of work, though could end up helping to boost your income and give you a challenge in a different field that you usually work in. Now I'm not saying jump into the first idea you have, but do some research and see if there is something out there that interests you, and whether you can see yourself having fun learning how to set this side-business up.

I think the number one rule if you decide to go down this route is not to be afraid of failing. It is highly likely it is going to take you several tries to figure out what works and what doesn't. The best businesses always go through several iterations before they get the right formula. I know this for myself as I've had a couple of failed attempts of starting a side business, but I haven't let that deter me, and I'm constantly on the lookout for the next challenge. You should also note that you won't make millions straight away; all the successful businesses take years of operation before they 'make it'. So if you are looking for some quick, easy cash, this isn't for you.

> **Please note**
>
> *There are a lot of paid influencers on social media that try to 'sell' side hustles as a get cash easy scheme. Remember though that money doesn't come easy, so it is always best to do your own research into an area before investing anything. Always start small and expand only if it becomes profitable. I highly recommend learning a bit about running a business such as how to read balance sheets or produce cashflow forecasts before starting just so that you can stay on top of what you are earning.*
>
> ***And please remember, this book is NOT investment advice!***

20. Go out Clubbing
(If you are the legal age to do so)

Let your hair down and go out clubbing. If clubbing isn't your scene then you can still do this one but by going out to a bar or a pub for some drinks instead. Now I personally wouldn't do this in the first 3 weeks after a break-up because it is more than likely you will end up drunk and crying in the street trying to call your ex (not that I've done this of course!). By going out you can enjoy the freedom of getting drunk with friends, dancing and possibly flirting with some strangers. Before you start downing those shots and getting the evening underway, I thought I'd highlight a couple of things you might want to do to make sure you have a safe and enjoyable night:

1. Firstly, make sure you don't have access to your ex's contact number. This means finally deleting it from your phone. If you are not ready to remove them completely from your life, then I recommend you write the number down on a piece of paper so you could always put it back in if you wanted to. The reason for doing this is so that you don't end up calling or texting them once you've had one too many, and it reduces the chances of you doing or saying something that you would regret in the morning.

2. Log-out of all your social media. Now I understand that this may seem a bit extreme for a lot of you, especially when you want to be posting pictures of the night out. The aim of this is to decrease the chances of 'drunk you', from messaging or stalking your ex during the night. Doing this can only bring

your mood down and ruin your evening, as you will only be opening old wounds by doing so. If you want to post pictures of your night out, there is nothing stopping you from doing it the next morning when you are a bit more sober and won't go looking at your ex's social media accounts.

3. Make sure you have a friend who is there to help get you home at the end of the night. You may well be capable of getting home safely by yourself at the end of a normal night out, but unfortunately the heartbreak you're currently feeling may lead you to drink a lot more than you usually would. Having someone there with you, who you can trust to comfort you and make sure you get back okay (without that detour to your ex's house) will mean you won't have to worry about something bad happening on the way home.

Please note

Make sure you thank said friend and possibly get them a drink next time you're out!

4. Finally, just have fun! You are out to have a good time with your friends, so relax and enjoy the evening.

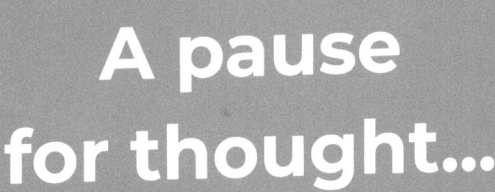

A pause for thought...

You may be feeling that you want your ex back and wondering why none of these activities are helping you to get them back. I ask that you take some time to heal, and to find who you are as a person before you start looking at ways of getting them back. I can't guarantee that the feeling of missing them will ever go away, but as time goes on that feeling will subside, especially if you start rebuilding a life that you want to live. If you use this opportunity to develop yourself, you will slowly come to the realisation that the time you had together was special, but in the long run they weren't meant to be the one that you spend the rest of your life with. You will find another partner who is more suited to your needs, and the kind of relationship that you want to have. Life has given you an opportunity to explore new paths, and you would be doing yourself a favour if you took this opportunity to explore what is out there.

I think the hard truth is that you wouldn't be in this situation if your ex really wanted to be with you, so don't waste your life waiting for someone who didn't want to be with you. Out of the seven billion people on this planet, there is at least one person (if not more) who will have the same values as you, and who would want to have you in their life.

21. Listen to music

You probably have already been listening to a lot of sad songs lately and probably feel as though this is how it's supposed to be after a break-up. Music is a powerful medium to convey emotions and unfortunately that means it can affect our moods more than we would like. By listening to those sad songs you have gotten yourself stuck in a loop which is not doing your mood any good, and it won't get you through the heartbreak any quicker. When I say listen to music, I mean listen to any other music genre apart from sad love songs. Listening to more upbeat music will hopefully allow you to feel a bit happier and get you to stop reminiscing about your last relationship. You never know, you may even find a new artist or band that you really enjoy listening to in the process.

22. Grow some plants

Developing some green fingers can be a great way for you to find a new hobby, as well as brighten up your room/home. If you are like me, and you aren't the best at keeping plants alive, then I would recommend planting a species that doesn't need much looking after (maybe a cactus or two). If you are good at watering and generally looking after plants, then you have a large selection of plants to choose from.

Another plus to growing plants is that it can be a good way for you to get outside and enjoy the fresh air (unless it's the dead of winter, in which case make yourself a hot chocolate and curl up on the sofa). If you don't have any outside space, growing and nurturing some indoor house plants will have the same positive effects. Looking after plants can be a really relaxing thing to do when you want some downtime. You can chuck on a podcast or some music, and get absorbed in looking after this thing that you want to grow.

23. Learn/improve your cooking

Why wouldn't you want to eat better tasting food?

Learning to cook will not only give you very useful life-skill, but it will help you explore new dishes that you would never normally eat. If you already cook a bit, then use this opportunity to learn some new dishes, and maybe even a different way to cook your meals. Unfortunately, when you are heartbroken, you can find yourself falling into a rut of cooking easy meals and not really making an effort in what you are eating. Eating a nicely cooked meal will help you get out of this rut.

As well as helping you improve your health, cooking can be a great way to distract yourself from how you are feeling about your ex. By focusing on the recipes to be proud of once you have finished cooking the meal. Cooking doesn't require you to follow recipes to the letter. I enjoy experimenting with the dishes that I make. **Yes**, you may not get the flavours right the first time, but by being creative you could end up making your own spin on the dish that your family and friends end up raving about. I can tell you that no matter how heartbroken you might be feeling, a good homemade meal can help you feel a bit better and lessen the pain you are feeling.

24. Sing

We aren't all Beyonce, but this shouldn't stop you from giving this one a go. The aim of this isn't to be pitch perfect, or to create the single of the year; simply to lose yourself in some music you enjoy listening to and to have some fun. Find yourself a song or two that you know the words to, then turn the sound up and sing along. If you are like me and you don't like the idea of doing this in front of people, then find an empty room, or just do it when you are driving between hobbies/work, where you won't need to worry about anyone listening in to what you are doing.

I'm not one to sing in front of other people (mainly because I'm a bit out of tune and I wouldn't want to punish anyone by making them hear me sing). However, when summer rolls around, I have my windows down and sing to some country songs that I have lined up on my playlist. The more that you sing out loud, whether this is by yourself or not, you will learn not to care what people think of you, and hopefully give you that little bit of confidence. That will in turn push you to new things that take you outside of your comfort zone.

25. Go to the beach

This is one of my favourite places to spend the summer, and if I could, I would be writing this book from there. Though the English sea is not the warmest of places to go swimming (and even during the hot summers it can feel like the Arctic Ocean), visiting the beach is a good way to get some fresh air and give yourself a change of scenery. As with anything based around nature, the good weather cannot be guaranteed all year round. However, going to the beach on the coldest, wettest or even an overcast day can instil a sense of peace and calm. You may not be able to go for a swim or sunbathe, but you will be able to go on some nice walks and explore the cities, towns or villages that perch on the edge of the coast.

> **A hot tip**
>
> *If you go in spring to autumn is to find yourself a nice bar/restaurant/chippy that overlooks the beach and watch the sunset whilst enjoying good food and/or drink.*

26. Listen to a podcast

Listening to music can sometimes get a bit boring, especially when you start hearing the same songs come up over and over again. Putting on a podcast can not only break this cycle, but you can also use it as an opportunity to learn something new, or to have something funny to listen to. The plus side of listening to podcasts is that you can open yourself up to different points of view, on topics that you wouldn't normally be exposed to. This will broaden the depth of your knowledge, and may lead you to becoming interested in a new subject matter. With the wide variety of genres and topics now available, you should hopefully be able to find something that stands out to you.

If you are currently feeling upset and down about the end of your last relationship, and are unsure about how to deal with your ex or to get back into the dating scene, I recommend listening to 'Love life with Matthew Hussey'. It helped me to understand what was happening from a new perspective, and allowed me to focus on how to learn from what I've just gone through to improve myself ready for when I jumped back into the dating pool. Hopefully if you are able to listen to this podcast or something similar, it will help you deal with what you are feeling, as well as helping you with any issues that you are having with dating.

27. Take up yoga

Challenge yourself to reach Zen by taking up yoga. Yoga is a good way for you to not only stretch out your muscles and do some exercise, but also a way for you to become part of a group of people who hold the same mindset. There are many different types of yoga that you can do, so it would definitely be worth looking into which form you think will work best for you. As well as being good for your body, yoga can help you focus and clear your mind of any stresses that have occurred during the day. Clearing your head of all stresses is a good starting point to help you begin to shape the journey that you want your life to follow. It can also help you to get clarity on events that may have occurred during the past.

28. Get fit

One of the great ways to get back at your ex and to get your confidence back that I would highly recommend is joining a gym or just getting back into shape. We all know that when you are in a relationship you may get a bit lazy, and start neglecting exercise because you're not needing to impress your partner anymore. I admit I fell into this trap! Getting your fitness back will not only help your physical and mental health, but feeling fitter will give you confidence when you get yourself back out into the dating scene, or achieve other goals you have in life. If you want to join a gym and don't really know what you are doing, ask the gym if there is a personal trainer who can help you work out a training plan, and to show you some exercises to start with. There is no harm asking other gym goers or athletes for some pointers in achieving what you have set out to achieve, they are often more than happy to help you.

On-top of the health benefits that exercising can give you, you can also channel the pain that you are feeling into something productive and use it as a driving force to push yourself harder with each session you do. Now with doing anything new, or getting back into it, you aren't going to see results straight away, it can take a couple of months before you see any physical improvement. To make progress you may also need to start eating healthier as your body will need to be fuelled properly in order to perform. Also making sure you get a good night's sleep is important so that your body can recover fully.

29. Go out for Brunch

This is probably one of my new favourite things to do and I'm a bit ashamed that I didn't start doing this sooner, but going out for brunch is a great excuse to get together with your friends and make some much needed new memories. Who can deny that going out for good food, having some drinks (whether they are alcoholic or non-alcoholic) and trading funny stories, is the best way to spend the weekend?

You don't need to have friends to go and do brunch. If no-one is available, go out by yourself, and get your book out as if you were going out for dinner by yourself. The whole idea is to have something that is going to get you out of the house and make new memories which you can look back on and smile at. You never know, you could end up creating a new Saturday or Sunday tradition that you enjoy doing with your mates.

30. Care less about how people see you

This one is easier said than done and will take a lot of practice to do. Sometimes it can seem like everyone is so focused on how they come across to others that they end up making themselves miserable. With the advent of social media, FOMO (Fear of Missing Out) runs wild in people's brains, they live less how they want to live, more a conceptualised version they see online. Do the activities you want to do, dress how you would like to dress. People will always say things about you and unfortunately that is just the way that society has evolved.

This will take time to develop and it will be hard to get to the point where you are confident enough not to care how other people view you. Trust me, it has taken twenty five and a half years to get to a version of myself where I can do things without second guessing what people think of me, and I am still learning not to worry what other people think of me. You will find that by doing this you will start living your life how you want to.

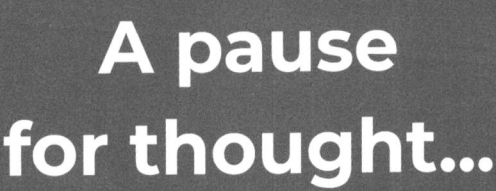

A pause for thought...

Family and friends will tell you after a break-up that there is nothing you need to change about yourself and that you are 'perfect' the way you are. I believe that is dangerous for our own development. We should always strive to learn from what has happened in our relationship and how we can build on it for when we get into our next relationship. Even if there is nothing we can learn from the last relationship (which is very unlikely as nothing is ever perfect), you should use this time to develop more hobbies, improve your physical or mental health, and to align spiritually with who you are. By improving who we are, we can learn what we want from future relationships, and it will also mean that you can achieve what you want from your goals in life.

31. Create a photo album

Everyone has a roll of photos on their phone which they never look at, but want to keep as they hold key memories. So why not make those photos more accessible to look at and put them in a photo album?

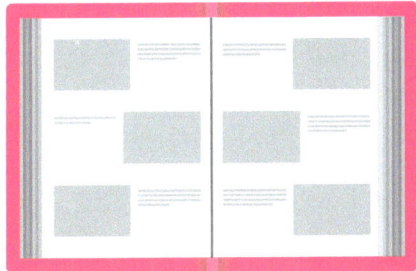

Having a photo album will allow you to flick through a physical book of the events that have occurred during your lifetime, and means that you can easily look through them without having to stare at your phone. Sorting through these images and putting them into the photo album can help you to see all the good things that have happened during your life, and how much fun you have had being single. Going forward you will be able to expand your photo album with new memories, so that when you are old and looking back on the 'good ol days', you have something to remind you of what happened.

32. Have a Spa day

Everyone needs time to relax and to take time to get away from the stresses of everyday life. Going for a spa day will not only allow you to relax in a calming environment, but can give you an excuse to get that massage, or treatment you have been thinking about. The other advantage of having a spa day is that you can always extend it to a weekend away. Something you should keep in mind, especially if this is the first time you have taken a break since the break-up, is that you may start to miss or regret what happened between you and your ex. It's important to accept that you are feeling this way and not to be too hard on yourself. Going from being busy to doing nothing gives the mind time to bring up feelings you thought you had buried. These will fade just as quickly as they came back.

33. Go for a drive

If you are going to do this activity please abide by the laws of the road and be considerate of other road users. No one likes a dangerous driver, and being heartbroken isn't an excuse for being one. Also I don't want the police knocking on my door citing this book as the reason for the increase of driving accidents.

Now the health and safety bit is out of the way, driving can be a good way for you to clear your head, as well as finding new places to explore. When I say go for a drive I don't mean go for a cross country drive to escape from what has just happened (though it might be something to add to the bucket list as it can be a good holiday idea). But rather go out for an hour or two and make sure that you head into the country rather than staying in the city. This will allow you to drive on quieter roads, as well as being able to appreciate the scenery that you are driving through. If you go through any towns or villages that have a place to get a coffee or some food, take advantage and explore them, as you may find some new experiences that you could take advantage of in the future.

Heartbreak Survival Guide

Now you are probably wondering how driving can help clear your head. The answer is that by driving, you will need to be putting all your focus into the driving itself, which in turn will distract you from what you are thinking or feeling. What I have found is that driving gives you the opportunity to cut away from the fog that may have been brought on by those thoughts and feelings, allowing you to come back to them with a new perspective so that you can sort through them in a healthier way.

34. Dance

When I say dance I don't mean go and join a dance class, though if that is your sort of thing then please go ahead. What I mean by dance is to chuck on those feel good old bangers that you have always loved, crank the sound up, and dance around your house. There is nothing more freeing than being able to dance how you like in a comfortable environment, without caring what anyone thinks. If you can't exactly play music out loud then put some headphones on. I'm afraid there are no excuses why you can't do this one, and I have been caught a couple of times trying to "dance" whilst I cook.

So why dance? Well dancing is a really good way to express emotions, as well as acting as a low impact form of exercise. Though you aren't going to be burning many calories, or gaining lots of muscles with the type of dancing we are talking about here, you will still get the same sort of happy chemicals and hormones that are released during exercise. This can help to improve your mood, and help you with moving on. Dancing is also a good way of expressing emotion, and will allow you to bring out how you are feeling at the time without having to open up to somebody (though I highly recommend you do this if it is possible).

35. Learn to forgive your ex

This is going to be a hard one and I am still working on this one myself as I write this book. Forgiving your ex isn't for them, and isn't saying that they get away scot free for what has happened, or how they treated you. The aim is to allow you to get the peace of mind that the relationship just wasn't for you. When I say forgive them, I'm not saying that you should forgive and tell them that you forgive them and become best friends. Rather acknowledging this to yourself. It will go a long way to helping you get through the heartbreak and the healing process.

Forgiveness is a way for you to see that your ex has flaws like any human. Their actions do not represent you in any way, and the relationship will have had good times at points. Holding onto anger, resentment and regret is a waste of your emotional energy and will only hold you back from developing further as a person. It is the final bit of closure you need for yourself in order to move on from the relationship.

36. Go stand up paddle boarding (SUP)

If you love water based activities then I highly recommend you try SUP. Not only will you get a bit of a workout, but it is something that will allow you to enjoy the sea or riverways near you. Now I must stress that with any water based activity there is some risk, so please make sure you can swim before doing it, and make sure you wear the correct safety equipment when you go out.

This activity is something that you can do by yourself or with friends and can allow you to explore the area you are currently staying or to look at new areas. When I did SUP with a mate in the weeks following my last break-up, I found it relaxing to be able to clear my head and enjoy the countryside that I live in. If you are new to SUP I recommend you start off doing it on a river or some form of sheltered water so that you can get a feel for getting your balance on the board while paddling. It can be a bit tricky getting used to balancing on the board whilst paddling with waves knocking you off most of the time!

37. Reconnect with your friends

Unfortunately a lot of friendships end up taking a backseat, especially in the early stages of a new relationship. This is not anyone's fault, and is perfectly normal as you inevitably end up putting a lot of energy and time into the start of a relationship. This can sometimes be exacerbated if things unfortunately start to deteriorate in the relationship, as you end up trying your best to keep things together. When you start to heal from your relationship, this is the best time to reach out to your friends and try to rebuild the connections. Though this shouldn't compromise the person who you want to become.

If you are reading this and thinking that you didn't lose any connections with your friends, then good on you. That doesn't mean you shouldn't reach out and try to organise doing more things with them though. As with any relationships you have in your life, whether it's with yourself, family or friends, you need to put the time in to make them work, and being newly single is a better time than any. Especially with all the time you now have at your disposal.

Alternatively if you did end up putting friendships on hold a bit, try not to beat yourself up about it. I ended up doing that myself in my last relationship, and as much as I regret doing that, I know moving forward into any new relationships, I need to put more time into maintaining the friendships that I have, and not putting them on hold for a new love interest. The only advice I can give you, if you were careless like myself, is to put the time in with your friends when you can. If you want to go out for a quick pint down the pub or go and explore somewhere, invite your friends along, and slowly you will be able to get your friendships back to a level that they once were. Remember that people only put the same amount of time into seeing you as you put into seeing them.

38. Find a motto to live by

This may seem airy fairy to a lot of you and I would have agreed with you about this before I started to write this book. By finding a mantra/motto to live by you can have something short and sweet to help you through those difficult times. If we are being honest, life is not a sunny summer day all the time. It is littered with storms which are there to challenge you and to mould you as a person. Whether these challenges are for better or worse, having something there that can help you keep track of what your values are will help ground you.

I have surprised myself by how mottos have helped me, whether it is out training for the next race, or whether it is to shift my perspective on how I was dealing with my break-up. They have helped me to realise what I stood for and what I need to do to get back up to the standards I wanted to hold myself at. Don't worry if it takes you a while to find a motto to live by. The important thing is just to have it in your support system should you ever need it in the future.

39. Take yourself on a date

To put it bluntly, you can't expect anyone else to love you unless you love yourself. So take yourself out on a date, whether it is one of the activities mentioned in this book or something different. You will find that by taking yourself out on dates you will learn more about yourself, as well as being able to have fun doing things that maybe your friends don't want to do. To get the full-effect when doing this, make sure you treat yourself as you would a date. Get the good seats in the cinema, or go for a nice bottle of wine if you take yourself out for some food.

Now I'm not saying you should put off dating other people just to date yourself. However, you can get fatigued trying to date a new person every week, as you have to put the best version of yourself forward and try to figure out if there is a connection between the two of you. Use dating yourself as a circuit breaker to these other dates. It can give you a chance to act as yourself, and give you a chance to recharge before you get back into the dating arena.
It will also help you start to practise self-care and to treat yourself to new experiences when they come along.

40. Finally, take care of yourself

The final activity I suggest, to help you survive and get over a breakup, is to take care of yourself. At the end of the day, by looking after yourself, you will find that your mental and physical health will return to levels that will allow you to enjoy the adventures life has in-store for you. It will also help you set a benchmark by which any potential future partners will have to measure up against. Try to be the best version of yourself, and then if they start to threaten this benchmark, you have an indicator to show you that maybe that person isn't compatible for yourself.

Just remember that a vast majority of the population experience heartbreak at some point in their lives. Even though taking care of yourself might not lessen the pain as quickly as you might hope, it will help you build a resilience that can help you should you ever get into the same situation again.

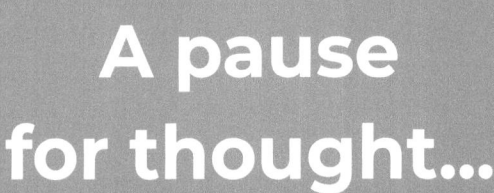

A pause for thought...

You are probably wondering whether it's a good idea to still be friends with your ex after breaking-up with them? Unfortunately there is a lot of conflicting information out there which doesn't really help with answering this question. I unfortunately can't answer this for you either as you need to decide who you want to have in your life and whether having them in your life is actually going to be good for you or whether allowing them into your life is just prolonging the pain.

As I've been on both sides of a break-up, I can give you what I think on this matter (again this is personal opinion, so please take it with a pinch of salt). I don't think that it's a good idea to be friends with your ex. Now you could still be friendly towards them and be at the same events as them, however being friends if not close friends will just lead to one or both party members not being able to move on. You have to remember that there is a motive for the person who broke up with you wanting to 'stay friends' so they can lessen the guilt they feel. Whilst if you were broken up with you hope that there is a chance you could 'win' them back, which will only stop you from moving on and getting the most out of your life. You also have to remember how your future partner might feel with you still being friends with your ex and would you like it if you were in their shoes.

If you are going to ignore this advice then I suggest you do these several things, so that both parties don't open any healed wounds.

1. Go no contact for a period. This is hard but getting a month of no contact can help you start working on yourself and allow you to figure out what you want from life.

2. Set boundaries and stick to them. If the opposite party violates these boundaries then you know that being friends isn't going to work.

3. Don't mention the past relationship and any issues that there were. Bringing up past issues will not only bring back old wounds. It also means that you aren't truly ready to forgive them and so a friendship shouldn't be started at this stage.

4. Limit the amount you hangout with them at the beginning. You aren't dating this person anymore, so limit yourself to seeing them once every 2 weeks and build it up as the new friendship grows. You should treat it like a meeting and become friends with a stranger.

5. Finally, don't do anything that you're not comfortable with.

I hope these tips can help you should you want to try and stay friends with your ex.

Some final thoughts...

I hope this survival guide has helped you while you recover from the break-up, and if you have gotten to the end and not seen any change, just remember that healing takes time. As you start to learn more about who you are as a person, the impact of the heart-break will lessen. Eventually you will find someone new who will treat and love you the way that you deserve. If there is one thing that I want you to do is to keep the **hope** you have, burning bright.

Whether or not you want to have a relationship moving forward, the most important thing you can do is to love yourself the way that you deserve, and to follow the journey in life that you want to take. As long as you live each day to the fullest, you will find yourself being able to do things that you could only dream about in the past.

Activity checklist

Use this checklist to help you keep track of the things you have completed within this book. You can also use the spaces at the end to record any idea of things that you think will help move forward out of your heartbreak.

- ○ Watch some movies
- ○ Unfollow your ex on all social media
- ○ Spend some time and work out who you are
- ○ Limit your social media use
- ○ Go for a daily walk
- ○ Buy some new clothes and get a new haircut
- ○ Meet-up with your friends
- ○ Plan a holiday
- ○ Join some new groups
- ○ Pull silly faces at yourself in the mirror
- ○ Join a dating app (18+)
- ○ Read some books
- ○ Learn mindfulness
- ○ Go out for a meal by yourself
- ○ Have a clear-out
- ○ Allow time to embrace your feelings
- ○ See a therapist about how you're feeling
- ○ Set yourself a goal

- ○ Start a side-business
- ○ Go out Clubbing
- ○ Listen to music
- ○ Grow some plants
- ○ Learn/improve your cooking
- ○ Sing
- ○ Go to the beach
- ○ Listen to a podcast
- ○ Take up yoga
- ○ Get fit
- ○ Go out for Brunch
- ○ Care less about how people see you
- ○ Create a photo album
- ○ Have a Spa day
- ○ Go for a drive
- ○ Dance
- ○ Learn to forgive your ex
- ○ Go stand up paddle boarding (SUP)
- ○ Reconnect with your friends
- ○ Find a motto to live by
- ○ Take yourself on a date
- ○ Finally, take care of yourself

Acknowledgements

This book wouldn't have come into fruition if it wasn't for the support of a select group of people, so as any good author would I thought I'd give them a shoutout, and say a quick thank you for what they have done (don't worry I'll make sure to buy them a round next time we're out).

Sally and Andy:
Thank you for helping with the proofing of this book and the support you have given me during the writing of this book. Without you this book wouldn't have made sense, and my readers would probably have put this down after reading the first page.

David, Ryan, Karis, Ashton and Libbi:
Thank you for being there and supporting me during the challenging times I went through. As well as helping me discover who the real 'Sam' is.

My pet cats:
Thank you for distracting me from writing this book by demanding cuddles.

www.ingramcontent.com/pod-product-compliance
Lightning Source LLC
Chambersburg PA
CBHW041512010526
44118CB00006B/233